BLUE BANNER
BIOGRAPHY

Blake
LIVELY

Joanne Mattern

Mitchell Lane
PUBLISHERS

P.O. Box 196
Hockessin, Delaware 19707
Visit us on the web: www.mitchelllane.com
Comments? email us: mitchelllane@mitchelllane.com

Mitchell Lane
PUBLISHERS

Printing   1   2   3   4   5   6   7   8   9

Blue Banner Biographies

Akon
Alicia Keys
Allen Iverson
Ashanti
Ashlee Simpson
Ashton Kutcher
Avril Lavigne
Beyoncé
Blake Lively
Bow Wow
Brett Favre
Britney Spears
Carrie Underwood
Chris Brown
Chris Daughtry
Christina Aguilera
Christopher Paul Curtis
Ciara
Clay Aiken
Cole Hamels
Condoleezza Rice
Corbin Bleu
Daniel Radcliffe
David Ortiz
David Wright
Derek Jeter
Drew Brees
Eminem
Eve
Fergie

Flo Rida
Gwen Stefani
Ice Cube
Ja Rule
Jamie Foxx
Jay-Z
Jennifer Lopez
Jessica Simpson
J. K. Rowling
Joe Flacco
John Legend
Johnny Depp
Justin Berfield
Justin Timberlake
Kanye West
Kate Hudson
Keith Urban
Kelly Clarkson
Kenny Chesney
Kristen Stewart
Lady Gaga
Lance Armstrong
Leona Lewis
Lil Wayne
Lindsay Lohan
Mariah Carey
Mario
Mary J. Blige
Mary-Kate and Ashley Olsen

Megan Fox
Miguel Tejada
Missy Elliott
Nancy Pelosi
Natasha Bedingfield
Orianthi
Orlando Bloom
P. Diddy
Peyton Manning
Pink
Queen Latifah
Rihanna
Robert Pattinson
Ron Howard
Sean Kingston
Selena
Shakira
Shia LaBeouf
Shontelle Layne
Soulja Boy Tell 'Em
Stephenie Meyer
Taylor Swift
T.I.
Timbaland
Tim McGraw
Toby Keith
Usher
Vanessa Anne Hudgens
Zac Efron

Library of Congress Cataloging-in-Publication Data
Mattern, Joanne, 1963–
  Blake Lively / by Joanne Mattern.
      p. cm. — (Blue banner biographies)
  Includes filmography.
  Includes bibliographical references and index.
  ISBN 978-1-58415-909-4 (library bound)
  1. Lively, Blake—Juvenile literature. 2. Actors—United States—Biography. I. Title.
  PN2287.L476M38 2010
  791.4502'8092—dc22
  [B]

2010011979

ABOUT THE AUTHOR: Joanne Mattern is the author of more than 250 books for children. She has written biographies about many famous people for Mitchell Lane, including *Ashley Tisdale, Peyton Manning, The Jonas Brothers, LeBron James,* and *Drake Bell and Josh Peck.* Joanne also enjoys writing about animals, reading, and being outdoors. She lives in New York State with her husband, four children, and several pets.

PUBLISHER'S NOTE: The following story has been thoroughly researched, and to the best of our knowledge represents a true story. While every possible effort has been made to ensure accuracy, the publisher will not assume liability for damages caused by inaccuracies in the data and makes no warranty on the accuracy of the information contained herein. This story has not been authorized or endorsed by Blake Lively.

PLB

Blue Banner Biography

In just a few years, Blake Lively rose from an unknown high school student to one of the most glamorous and popular stars on television and in movies.

A Family Favor

Blake Lively was just doing her brother a favor. Eric Lively had been bugging his little sister to become an actress. When Blake was just fifteen years old, Eric had taken her on a two-month tour of Europe. He spent a lot of the time trying to convince her that she should become an actor, just like he was. "He was trying to get me to make life decisions at fifteen!" Blake recalled with a laugh to *W* magazine a few years later.

At first, Blake said she wasn't interested, but Eric would not take no for an answer. He gave Blake's photo to his agent and told the agent to recommend her for auditions. "I would have these agents calling and saying, 'We have an appointment for you.' It was really hard to say no, because I didn't want to make my brother upset."

To make Eric happy, Blake did try out for a few parts. Then, in 2004, sixteen-year-old Blake went on her third audition. It was for *The Sisterhood of the Traveling Pants*, a movie based on a popular novel of the same title. It told the story of four girlfriends who are linked by a pair of jeans that magically fits each one of them. Three of the roles had

Blake grew up in a privileged family, but she is always happy to use her celebrity to raise money for charity. When she was just becoming famous, she appeared at an event to benefit Project Angel Food.

already been cast when Blake auditioned. She was trying out for the part of Bridget, an athletic girl with a troubled past who is going away from home for the first time.

Blake walked into the audition and gave her photo to the casting directors. The directors turned over the photo, expecting to see a list of Blake's acting credits on the back. To their surprise, the paper was completely blank. Blake did not have one acting credit to her name, yet here she was, trying out for a lead role in a major motion picture.

Blake did not let her lack of experience make her nervous. She picked up the script and read the scenes the directors asked her to. Then she thanked them for their time and left the room.

After she left, the directors could not stop talking about her. They knew she was exactly the actress they were looking for to play the role of tough yet insecure Bridget. They quickly called her agent and offered her the part.

The Sisterhood of the Traveling Pants was the start of Blake Lively's career. In just a few years, she went from an actress with no experience to one of the most popular and hardworking stars on television.

> *After [Blake] left, the directors could not stop talking about her. They knew she was exactly the actress they were looking for.*

A Hollywood Family

*B*lake Lively was born on August 25, 1987, in Tarzana, California. Although her family was thrilled about her birth, they were also surprised. All the doctors had told Blake's parents that they were having a boy. They had picked out the name Blake to honor an uncle who had that name. When it turned out the tests were wrong, Ernie and Elaine Lively could not think of calling the baby anything besides Blake. They named her Blake Christina Lively.

Baby Blake was the newest addition to a large show-business family. Ernie was an actor who had appeared in more than 100 television shows. Some of his credits include *The X-Files*, *The West Wing*, and *The Ghost Whisperer*. He also taught acting classes to young adults, several of whom went on to be major stars.

Elaine Lively was also involved in show business. She posed as a swimsuit model for several major magazines. She also works as an acting coach and manager. Elaine was married before, and has three children from that first marriage. Their names are Lori, Jason, and Robyn, and they are all actors, too.

Blake is the youngest child of a close-knit Hollywood family. Her mother (right) and father joined her at the premiere of one of her movies in 2008.

Ernie and Elaine had a son named Eric, who is six years older than Blake. Eric has modeled for major clothing companies and appeared on many television shows.

Blake was always around other actors when she was growing up. Her parents did not want to leave her with a baby-sitter, so they took her to work with them all the time. "I grew up in their acting classes, watching other people, so I was always learning and absorbing," Blake told *Allure* magazine. "I was prepped my whole life for acting without realizing it."

Blake was a shy child, and she believes that being around other actors was good for her. "It really helped. I would've just been hiding under the table, pulling on my mother's dress, if I hadn't been in their classes. It forced me out of my shell," she told *W* magazine.

> *"I was in a little pink silk bed and there were Mickey and Donald and Goofy looking down at me."*

Blake may have enjoyed being around other actors, but the experience didn't really encourage her to follow in their footsteps. "Because I was around it so much, I thought, Okay, this is what I don't want to do, rather than realizing, This is the perfect setup for what I should be doing."

Because Blake was so comfortable onstage and on movie sets, her parents thought she might like acting. In 1992, she auditioned for a part in a movie called *Mrs. Doubtfire*, in which Robin Williams would star as a divorced dad who dresses up as a female housekeeper in order to spend time with his children. Blake auditioned for the role of the youngest child in the family, but the part went to another actress, Mara Wilson.

Blake finally got a role in a movie, and it was a true family production. When she was ten years old, her father produced and directed a small film called *Sandman*. The movie was a fantasy for children, and Blake played two roles, the Tooth Fairy and a character named Trixie. Blake and her family had fun making the movie, but Ernie was not able to find a company to distribute the film, so *Sandman* was never released.

Blake was not very disappointed that the movie never appeared in theaters. She was having too much fun in real

Growing up in California, Blake often went to the beach with her friends. She tried surfing for the first time when she was thirteen but ended up breaking her nose. Still, the beach remained a favorite spot to sunbathe and swim throughout Blake's childhood and teenage years.

life. Her parents raised their child in an unusual way. Blake has told interviewers that she grew up at Disneyland.

Her first memory is from when she was three years old and she woke up in a Disneyland hotel. "I was in a little pink silk bed and there were Mickey and Donald and Goofy looking down at me," she told *Marie Claire*. "It was the most exciting place in the world."

Disneyland became almost a second home for Blake and her mother, who went to the theme park twice a week. "I did well in school, so I guess my mom just wanted to have some extra time to bond with me," Blake explained to *Marie Claire*.

"Sometimes, when I was older, she'd keep me out till one in the morning. We only stayed out late on weekends. We'd get a hotel room and then go to Denny's, drink coffee, and talk for hours. My mom tells the most amazing stories. In a way, she was kind of raising me to be a great actress without even realizing it."

School was also a different experience for Blake. She first went to school when she was only three years old. Eric did not want to go alone, so their mother enrolled her in first grade. "My mom told them I was six since I was so tall," Blake told *Marie Claire*. The experience did not go well for her. "After a few weeks they said they would have to put me in mentally disabled classes because I wasn't up to pace with the rest of the kids. They thought I was slow because all I wanted to do was sleep while the other kids were doing their projects. So my mom took me out of school."

"I had a lot of friends in high school, but I was never the wild party girl. Never have been, never plan to be!"

Blake attended thirteen different schools during her childhood. She was also homeschooled for a time. Finally, she settled into Burbank High School, where she was an active part of the student body. "I was really involved in my school. I was the only person to dress up on Spirit Days. No one had spirit, so I made up for everyone," she told *CosmoGirl*. She was also very popular without getting into trouble. "I had a lot of friends in high school, but I was never the wild party girl. Never have been, never plan to be!" she told *InStyle*. Acting was the farthest thing from Blake's mind—until her brother Eric had a different idea.

CHAPTER 3

A Sisterhood of Actresses

*B*lake and Eric were very close growing up. As Eric became more involved in his acting and modeling career, he believed that Blake would enjoy following the same path. He also thought that she should experience more of the world. When she was fifteen and in her sophomore year of high school, Eric took her on a very special trip. The brother and sister spent two months traveling around Europe. Instead of studying world history in school, Blake got to visit the places where history happened.

Eric also wanted Blake to think about her future. "He sat me down when we were in Europe and said, 'What are you going to do with your life?' I'm fifteen at the time. And so he made a chart of things I could possibly do, and nothing really interested me. And then a year later, he said, 'I think you're going to be an actress.' "

Blake completely disagreed. "I had no clue what I wanted to do, but I knew it was not acting—just because my whole family was in it, and it was the only job I really knew of," she explained.

Blake became good friends with her Traveling Pants *costars, (left to right) America Ferrera, Alexis Bledel, and Amber Tamblyn. The three older actresses were supportive of Blake as she made her first big movie.*

Despite her reservations, Eric asked his agent to set up some auditions for Blake, and she went to them. She was willing to try it, even if she didn't think it was the perfect choice for her.

In 2004, Blake tried out for a role in *The Sisterhood of the Traveling Pants.* She was not nervous about auditioning for such a major part. In fact, she was calmer than many other actresses who had more experience. "I got the job because I wasn't freaking out," she told *Allure.* "It wasn't like, 'I have to get this part, or my life is over.' " Her confidence and relaxed attitude impressed the film's casting directors, and so did her talent. She got the part. As an added bonus, Blake's father played her character's father in the movie.

Blake had a great time filming *The Sisterhood of the Traveling Pants*. She became good friends with the actresses playing the other three girls in the movie, Alexis Bledel, America Ferrera, and Amber Tamblyn. The girls filmed part of the movie in Vancouver, British Columbia, Canada, and Blake was happy to have companions who were older than she and treated her with respect. "Alexis, America, Amber, and I formed a really good friendship on the first *Sisterhood* movie," Blake told *Seventeen*. "I was in high school at the time, and a lot of times girls are insecure and aren't so nice to each other. So it was really refreshing to have three females who could help one another, who were happy for each other, and love each other."

> *The Sisterhood of the Traveling Pants was a big hit with both critics and audiences.*

After they filmed their scenes together in Canada, the actresses traveled to different locations to film other parts of the movie. Blake traveled to Mexico, where her character, Bridget, was attending a soccer camp. The scenes in Mexico were especially difficult for her, because although she had played soccer, she was not very good at it. Not one to back down from a challenge, she worked hard to become competent enough to pass for a great athlete.

The Sisterhood of the Traveling Pants was released in June 2005 and was a big hit with both critics and audiences. It earned more than $39 million. Suddenly, Blake Lively was a star! She was used to fans recognizing her parents and her brothers and sisters, but her own fame was much more overwhelming for her. All the attention was a little hard to get used to, but Blake's family helped her stay focused and didn't let her get carried away.

Blake was thrilled that the movie was so popular, but the success of *The Sisterhood of the Traveling Pants* forced her to make a difficult decision. She had not expected the movie to be such a big hit, and she had only taken the role to please her brother and because she wanted to try something new. Now everyone was telling her that she should quit school and become a full-time actress.

> "I was very involved in school: I was class president, . . . I was in cheerleading, I was in all AP classes, six different clubs. It was my life."

Blake wasn't sure this was the right thing to do. "Everybody was telling me, 'Oh, you can't go back to high school. You can't finish your senior year. You gotta keep doing movies now.' I was very involved in school: I was class president, I was in a nationally competitive show choir, I was in cheerleading, I was in all AP classes, six different clubs. It was my life."

Blake loved school too much to give it up. She decided to finish her senior year. Although she had planned to go to college and was accepted at Stanford University, she decided to take a year off after high school and see about becoming an actress. Maybe she could have the best of both worlds.

From Movies to Television

*A*s soon as she graduated from Burbank High School, Blake plunged into the life of a full-time actress. She quickly landed the role of Monica in another movie, *Accepted*. It is about a group of students who are not accepted by any of the colleges to which they apply. Instead, the friends, led by a character named Bartleby (Justin Long), start their own college. They soon find themselves on a mission to expose a nearby school as a sham. *Accepted* did well at the box office, and was nominated for two Teen Choice Awards.

After finishing *Accepted*, Blake took a role in a very different film, called *Simon Says*. This horror film is about a group of students who are terrorized by a crazed serial killer. Although Blake played one of the victims, she had a lot of fun making the movie, because it was a family affair. Blake's father produced the film, and he also appeared in the movie. So did Blake's sisters Robyn and Lori, her brother-in-law Bart Johnson, and her boyfriend at the time, fellow actor Kelly Blatz. *Simon Says* mixes horror with humor, and it received a good reception at the Brussels International Festival of

In the movie Accepted, *Blake's popular character learns an important lesson about being true to oneself from outsider Bartleby, played by Justin Long.*

Fantastic Film in 2007. It was never released in the United States, although some scenes were leaked onto the Internet.

At the end of 2006, Blake began filming a movie called *Elvis and Anabelle*. She was determined to try many different roles, and this movie gave her another chance to do something different. In the film, Blake plays Anabelle, a beauty queen who apparently dies after a pageant. She is revived by a kiss from a boy named Elvis, and the two become close. The experience helps Anabelle realize what she really wants out of life. The role was a very emotional and difficult part to play, and Blake worked hard to make her character's emotions believable. The movie received good reviews, and critics praised Blake's performance.

After *Elvis and Anabelle*, Blake had the opportunity to try something really different. At the time, producers Stephanie Savage and Josh Schwartz were developing a show based on the hugely popular teen book series called *Gossip Girl*. Like the books, the television series would focus on the lives of incredibly rich and spoiled teens who live in the exclusive Upper East Side neighborhood of New York City. Savage and Schwartz heard about Blake through online message boards, where fans kept recommending her for a part in the show.

Being on television can be hard work. Blake and her costars spend hours getting their hair and makeup styled before they step before the cameras to play their sophisticated and glamorous characters on Gossip Girl.

Blake is very different from her Gossip Girl *character, Serena. Although Blake has never been in trouble, Serena was arrested in one memorable scene on the show.*

When the producers offered Blake the part of Serena van der Woodsen, Blake was not sure she should take the job. She thought of herself as a serious movie actress, not someone who starred in a television soap opera! However, she liked how dedicated and involved Schwartz and Savage were. "They are so excited about what they do," she told BuzzSugar.com. "They are so passionate and so young, and they're not some jaded studio executive who just signs off their name for some commercial product . . . and is never involved. . . . If it wouldn't have been them, I definitely don't think I'd be doing the show."

Blake ended up loving her role as Serena. Her character had been in a lot of trouble and was sent away from home for a time. Now she is back and trying to find her place in a world full of temptations, while trying to learn from her mistakes and become a better person.

Blake has enjoyed everything about *Gossip Girl*. For one thing, the show is taped in New York City, a place Blake loves. She also loves wearing the high-fashion clothes that are such a big part of her character's lifestyle. "I think the real reason for Blake was the opportunity for clothing," Josh Schwartz told *W*. "I remember talking to her about that. She was like, 'Wait, so you're asking me to move to New York and wear the most incredible clothing, some of which you might actually let me keep?' "

"Wait, so you're asking me to move to New York and wear the most incredible clothing, some of which you might actually let me keep?"

Gossip Girl premiered on the CW Network in 2007 and was an instant hit. Fans loved this outrageous perception of the lives of the rich, and they enjoyed watching the characters face all sorts of dilemmas. The show became one of the most popular and notorious shows on television. Blake had found a role she could play for a long time.

*Blake is good friends with **Gossip Girl** costar Leighton Meester, even though tabloids like to try to stir up trouble between the two actresses.*

CHAPTER 5

Blake's Private Life

*E*ven while devoted to *Gossip Girl*, Blake found time to make several more movies. In 2008, she played Bridget once again in *The Sisterhood of the Traveling Pants 2*. She had a wonderful time reuniting with her former costars, America, Amber, and Alexis. In 2009, Blake made two movies, *The Private Lives of Pippa Lee* and *New York, I Love You*. In 2010, she began filming a crime drama called *The Town*, as well as an action film based on the comic book character the Green Lantern.

Gossip Girl has been the focus of Blake's life, and she's thrilled to spend her days on the set. She has always found friendships with her costars in the movies she's made, and the same is true of her costars on *Gossip Girl*. Leighton Meester, the former model who plays Blair Waldorf on *Gossip Girl*, has become a close friend of Blake's, even though their characters often fight on the show. Blake laughs at tabloid reports that she and Leighton do not get along. "It's absurd," she told *Cosmopolitan*. "We get along so well." She also told *W*, "I've never really had a competitive relationship in any work situation. The media is always trying to pit us against each other. I guess because it's just not interesting to say, 'Everyone gets along; everybody just works eighteen-hour days and goes home to sleep.' That's not fun to read, I guess."

Blake found a very special friendship with another costar, Penn Badgley, who plays Serena's boyfriend, Dan, on *Gossip Girl*. After just a few months of shooting the TV show together, Blake and Penn became a couple in real life. Although the two have been seen in public together many times and both admit to dating, Blake doesn't like to give many details of their relationship to the public. "We're putting so much of ourselves out there for the world, there are very few things that we have to ourselves, and my

After Blake met Penn Badgley on the set of Gossip Girl, *their friendship soon blossomed into romance. The two have often been spotted around New York City, enjoying their time together.*

Blake and Leighton Meester had fun appearing together on Total Request Live *in 2007. Blake and her* Gossip Girl *costars make many appearances to promote their hit television show.*

personal relationships—whether it's family or friends or the person you're in love with—that's your own, and I treasure that," she told *Allure*. "You see people who will open up their relationships . . . and their relationships just seem to crumble, so I decided to keep a vow of silence."

Blake also remains very close to her family and credits them with her success in both her personal and professional lives. She told *Seventeen*, "When I care about somebody, whether it's my best friend or somebody [I date], I give them all of my heart. I've just been so loved, and I'm used to really loving people and trusting them."

After Blake appeared as a presenter at the 2009 Golden Globes, she happily escorted her father to an after-party sponsored by InStyle *magazine and Warner Brothers Studios.*

She was devastated when her father was in a serious car accident in October 2008 and rushed home to be by his side. After he recovered, she brought him to the 2009 Golden Globe Awards as her guest. "I brought my dad because he'd had a tough year. I thought, Well, you were in a car that flipped six times—you should be at the Golden Globes!"

Blake is also happy to use her fame to help others. She has taken part in a number of charity events, including

Blake lends her star power to many charities, including a fashion industry charity event to help fund the fight against HIV/AIDS.

benefits for Gabrielle's Angel Foundation for Cancer Research and New Yorkers for Children, a charity that helps young people in foster care. Also in 2009, she partnered with Charity Water and Swarovski to create a crystal necklace. All the profits earned in the United States would fund clean water in developing nations.

> *"I think that I strive to do the right thing and not . . . get caught up in some of the nonsense. And I really try to steer clear of that."*

Blake knows that Serena, the character she plays on television, is often involved in dangerous behavior that is unacceptable for teenagers. Although Blake and Serena are very different, Blake sees one thing they have in common. As she explained to the Associated Press, "At the heart of it all, Serena really wants to be a good person — despite all odds, despite all the chaos that's going on around her and all the other people in her life. So I think that I strive to do the right thing and not fall into the norm like so many young people in Hollywood who — because they were raised differently — get caught up in some of the nonsense. And I really try to steer clear of that."

Blake's family gave her a strong foundation, both for her successful career and her happy life. She is an actress that many people love and admire. With her talent and generous spirit, Blake is likely to continue her winning streak for many years to come.

1987   Blake Christina Lively is born on August 25.

1992   Blake auditions for *Mrs. Doubtfire* but does not get the part.

1998   Blake appears in *Sandman,* a film directed by her father.

2002   She and her brother Eric travel around Europe.

2004   Blake is cast in *The Sisterhood of the Traveling Pants.*

2006   She graduates from high school and decides to take a year off to pursue acting. She is cast in *Accepted* and *Simon Says.*

2007   Blake appears in the film *Elvis and Anabelle;* she stars as Serena van der Woodsen in the TV show *Gossip Girl.*

2008   Blake appears in *The Sisterhood of the Traveling Pants 2.*

2009   She appears in *The Private Lives of Pippa Lee* and *New York, I Love You.*

2010   She begins filming *The Town* and *Green Lantern.*

2010   *Green Lantern*

        The Town

2009   *New York, I Love You*

        The Private Lives of Pippa Lee

2008   *The Sisterhood of the Traveling Pants 2*

2007   *Gossip Girl* (TV; ongoing)

        Elvis and Anabelle

2006   *Accepted*

        Simon Says

2005   *The Sisterhood of the Traveling Pants*

FURTHER READING

Books
Robin, Emily. *Blake Lively: Traveling to the Top.* New York: Scholastic, 2008.

Works Consulted
"Blake Lively Q&A." *CosmoGirl,* April 11, 2009.
http://www.blakelivelyweb.com/press/news.php?newsid=15
BuzzSugar. "Interview: Blake Lively of 'Gossip Girl.' " September 19, 2007.
http://www.buzzsugar.com/Interview-Blake-Lively-Gossip-Girl-640271
Chen, Eva. "Little Miss Sunshine." *Teen Vogue,* March 2008, pp. 218–221.
Fahner, Molly. "Everyone's Talking About Blake Lively." *Cosmopolitan,* September 2008, vol. 245, issue 3, pp. 52–56.
Hauser, Brooke. "The Girl Next Door." *Allure,* May 2009, pp. 180–185.
Miller, Rebecca. "Blake's Progress." *Marie Claire,* December 2009, vol. 16, issue 12, pp. 158–164.
Wood, Dana. "Lively Time." *W,* December 2008, pp. 280–283.

On the Internet
Blake Lively Source
http://www.blakelivelysource.com
Gossip Girl Cast and Crew
http://www.tv.com/gossip-girl/show/68744/cast.html
Gossip Girl Official Site
http://www.cwtv.com/shows/gossip-girl
Internet Movie Database: Blake Lively
http://www.imdb.com/name/nm05151161
Project Angel Food
http://www.angelfood.org

INDEX